Be the Best
SOCCER

Play Like a Pro

By Anthony Ventura

Troll Associates

Library of Congress Cataloging-in-Publication Data

Ventura, Anthony.
    Soccer, play like a pro / by Anthony Ventura.
      p.   cm.—(Be the best!)
    Summary: Examines the equipment, skills, and rules associated with
soccer.
    ISBN 0-8167-1933-0 (lib. bdg.)   ISBN 0-8167-1934-9 (pbk.)
    1. Soccer—Juvenile literature. [1. Soccer.] I. Title.
II. Series.
GV943.25.V46 1990
796.334'2—dc20   89-27292

Be the Best

SOCCER

Play Like a Pro

FOREWORD

by G. Peppe Pinton

Over the years, I have watched the world's most popular sport take off at the grassroots level. Now, it is a familiar sight in nearly every ball park. Youth soccer is especially growing, as more and more young people discover just how much fun and excitement this sport provides.

Soccer, Play Like a Pro, gives new players, their parents, and first-time coaches the basic knowledge they'll need for the game. It is not only valuable reference material, but also thoroughly enjoyable reading.

G. Peppe Pinton has been an executive with the New York Cosmos soccer organization since 1977. During this time, he has headed Soccer Camps of America, which operated the Pele Soccer Camps, the Franz Beckenbauer Soccer Camps, and the Cosmos Soccer Camps. In 1983, Peppe was both general manager and vice president of the Lazio soccer club in Italy's First Division. He has also been head soccer coach on both the high-school and college level in the United States.

Contents

Soccer's Family Tree

What is the most popular sport in the world? Did you guess soccer? If you did, you're right! Soccer is played and loved by millions of fans all over the globe.

In many countries, soccer is called football. "Football" is a good name for this sport. That's because to play soccer, a player must use his or her feet.

How did soccer become the world's most popular sport? It is a long story that begins more than two thousand years ago. Soccer was played by the ancient Greeks and Romans. It was also played in one form or another by the Chinese, the Japanese, and the Aztec Indians.

Early soccer was not always played with a ball. Sometimes a bag stuffed with straw or an air-filled animal's bladder was used.

Ancient soccer was not much like the modern sport. It was a rough and sometimes dangerous game. Nevertheless, more and more people began to play soccer as the years passed. The popularity of the game continued to grow.

Some English kings thought the game of soccer was *too* popular. They made it against the law to play soccer. These kings wanted the people to spend more time practicing archery. In those days, archery was more than just a sport. Soldiers used archery to defend their country. The kings believed shooting a bow well was more important than playing soccer.

But the game of soccer did not die out. In the Middle Ages, one town would play against another. Sometimes the contests were rough. To make the game safer, rules were drawn up and published in 1863. In the late 1880s, the rules were improved, and leagues were formed in different countries. Soccer had begun to resemble the game it is today.

Modern soccer has set rules and laws. They are the same in every country. The Fédération internationale de football association (the International Federation of Association Football) governs soccer. It includes the United States, which also has the United States Soccer Federation to oversee the sport.

Every four years, soccer teams from all over the globe compete in a famous soccer tournament. It is called the World Cup competition. The World Cup is the Super Bowl of soccer. To win the competition is a great honor. The winners are acknowledged as world champions.

Would you like to be a champion soccer player someday? With hard work and practice, perhaps you will.

What You Need
To Play Soccer

To play some sports, you need expensive equipment. Not soccer! Soccer is a simple game that can be played with very little equipment. That is one reason why soccer is so popular throughout the world. All you need to play soccer is a ball, a field, and some friends.

At each end of the field there is a goal. Teams score points in soccer by kicking the ball into their opponent's goal. But of course, that is not easy to do. Players must move the ball down the field past their opponents by using only their feet, foreheads, and bodies. Players are not allowed to use their hands or arms. Rough play, like pushing or tripping, is also not allowed.

The only player allowed to touch the ball with hands or arms is the goalie. The goalie stays in front of the goal area and stops the ball from scoring. It is a hard job. That is why goalies are allowed to use their hands.

GOAL AREA

A soccer game is filled with nonstop action and excitement. It is easy and fun to play. Even in regulation games there are only a few complicated rules. So becoming a soccer expert is not too hard. But becoming an expert soccer player is a lot harder. It takes patience and practice.

THE BALL

Any kind of medium-sized bouncing ball can be used to practice soccer. For practicing alone, even a tennis ball can be kicked around.

An official soccer ball is made of leather and weighs fourteen to sixteen ounces. It is covered with 32 five- and six-sided panels. Usually, most of the panels are white with some black ones. Occasionally, some soccer balls have red and blue panels instead of black. The panels help players judge the speed and direction of the ball as it spins in the air or on the field.

OFFICIAL SOCCER BALL

A leather soccer ball can take a lot of punishment. It will last a long time. It is one piece of soccer equipment worth buying.

THE FIELD

Any open field can be used for a neighborhood game. For safe play, a field should be level and without rocks or holes.

At each end of the field, mark off a goal area. Both goal areas must be the same size. (The smaller they are, the harder it is to score.) The goal-area lines are also the end lines of the field. Then side boundaries must be determined. Now the field is ready for action.

A regulation soccer field is 100 to 130 yards long. It is 50 to 100 yards wide.

An official field is separated by lines into special areas. There is a halfway line across the middle of the field. In the middle of the halfway line is the center circle. In the exact middle of that is the center spot. The side boundaries are called touchlines. At each end of the field are rectangles called penalty areas. Inside the penalty areas are the goal areas.

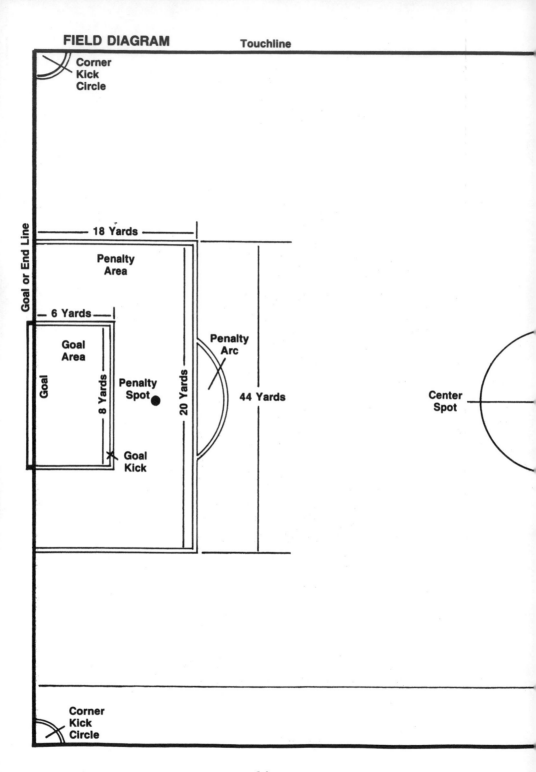

FIELD DIAGRAM

Touchline

Corner
Kick
Circle

Goal or End Line

18 Yards

Penalty
Area

6 Yards

Goal
Area

Goal

8 Yards

Penalty
Spot

20 Yards

Penalty
Arc

44 Yards

Goal
Kick

Center
Spot

Corner
Kick
Circle

14

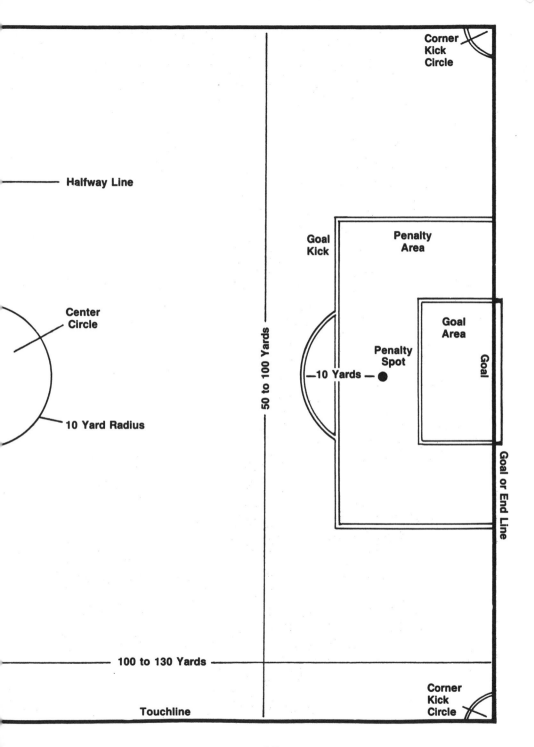

Corner
Kick
Circle

Halfway Line

Goal
Kick

Penalty
Area

Center
Circle

Goal
Area

Penalty
Spot

Goal

10 Yard Radius

—10 Yards —●

50 to 100 Yards

Goal or End Line

100 to 130 Yards

Corner
Kick
Circle

Touchline

15

In regulation play, the goal itself is eight yards wide and eight feet high. It is usually backed by a net. More about the purposes of these areas will be discussed in Chapter 8, "Tips on Regulation Play."

OTHER EQUIPMENT

Not much besides a field and a ball are needed to play soccer. Uniforms are usually matching shirts, shorts, and socks.

Special shoes are not necessary. Sneakers are fine for playing on a dry field. However, rubber-studded soccer shoes should be worn on soft or slippery turf.

Some soccer players also wear shin guards. Shin guards are long, hard plastic strips worn under knee socks. They protect a player's legs in case they're kicked.

16

Before You Begin

LIMBERING UP

Limbering up is sometimes called warming up or loosening up. It is a way to get blood flowing to the muscles you plan to use. It is also a way to stretch tense muscles so they will be loose and ready to work when you are.

Before doing any physical activity, limber up for ten to fifteen minutes. In colder weather, take a bit longer. Loosening up should always be done in a slow, easy fashion. Never hurry. A proper warm-up helps prevent muscle pulls and cramps.

EXERCISES

Warm-up exercises such as sit-ups, pushups, and jumping jacks are good ways to get blood flowing through the body. Slowly running in place is also good. Any exercises you enjoy can be used to warm up.

LIMBERING UP

Jumping Jacks

Slowly Running in Place

Pushups

STRETCHING

An important part of limbering up is stretching. Stretching loosens tight muscles. Remember, always stretch slowly.

One very good stretching exercise is the *crossed-leg toe touch*. It stretches the muscles in the back of the leg. To do it, cross one leg behind the other so your feet are almost side by side. Keeping the knees locked, slowly bend over and try to touch your toes. Reach down as far as you can go. Stop and hold that position for a few seconds. Rise, switch legs, and repeat the bending. As

STRETCHING

CROSSED-LEG TOE TOUCH

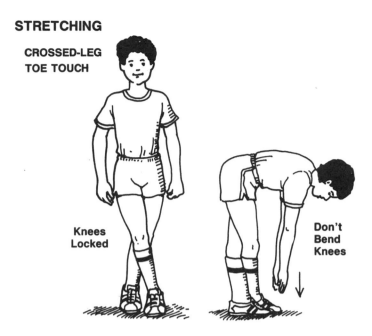

Knees Locked

Don't Bend Knees

you bend, you will feel the muscles in the back of your leg stretching.

Another good stretch is the *hurdler's stretch.* Sit on the ground. Keep one leg stretched out in front of you. Bend the other leg at the knee so your foot is behind you and to the side. Reach forward and try to touch your hand to your outstretched toe. Switch legs and repeat. Again, do this very slowly.

HURDLER'S STRETCH

CONDITIONING

Soccer is a nonstop running game. So it is important not to tire quickly. Running is one of the best ways to build your endurance.

When running, keep your body straight and balanced. Do not lean too far forward. Keep your feet pointed straight ahead. Try to make the front of each foot touch the ground first after each stride.

Pump your arms slowly in a comfortable fashion. Do not ball your hands into fists; you'll only reduce your speed and tire more quickly. Keep your hands open and relaxed. Breathe through your mouth and nose as you run. Try to keep your strides smooth so you glide along. Remember, no two people run exactly alike. Try to adapt these guidelines to the style that suits you best.

When running, do not overdo it. If you feel tired, stop and walk. Each day, run for a bit longer. If your muscles get very sore, take a day off. Muscles need rest, too.

Always pace yourself! It takes time to build up endurance. Give your body that time.

How to Develop
Soccer Skills

To play the game of soccer and play it well, you must acquire and develop certain skills. In all sports there is a right way and a wrong way to do things.

This section deals with the right way to perform certain soccer skills. Various ways of kicking, plus basic playing strategies such as passing, dribbling, and gaining control of the ball, will be covered.

Size is not a big factor in soccer. Little players are as good as big players. Girls and boys are equally skillful. In many organized leagues, girls and boys of all sizes play on the same team.

How good a player you become is mostly up to you. Hard work and practice are the keys to becoming a better soccer player.

KICKING THE BALL

Kicking is the one basic skill you need to play soccer. A kick at the goal is called a *shot.* A kick toward a teammate is called a *pass.* There are several kicks used to pass and shoot a soccer ball. When practicing soccer kicks, alternate your kicking foot. A soccer player must be able to kick with either foot.

As you kick, keep your eye on the ball. Do not just kick the ball aimlessly. Try to have a target in mind. That way, you will develop accuracy. And practice! The more you practice, the better you will become.

The Instep Kick The *instep,* or *low-drive, kick* is the most powerful soccer kick. The kick is made with the flat area across the top of your foot—where your shoelaces are.

INSTEP KICK

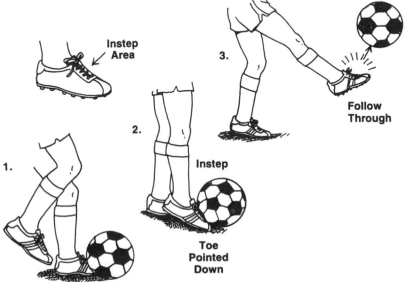

If you want the ball to travel on the ground, kick the ball at or above its center midpoint. If you want the ball to rise, kick it below its center midpoint.

To do the instep kick, bend your leg at the knee. Swing the foot backward, then forward. Also lean forward a bit. Keep your toes pointed at the ground, not at the ball. Strike the ball with the instep. Follow through by letting your leg continue to swing forward.

Another tip on keeping the instep kick low, which gives it power, has to do with the nonkicking foot. Place the nonkicking foot alongside the ball rather than behind it. That way, you will have proper balance and the ball will not sail upward.

INSTEP KICK

RIGHT!   WRONG!

First, practice the instep kick with a still ball while you are standing still. Once you master that, try running up to a still ball and kicking it. As you improve, practice kicking as you approach a ball rolling toward you.

The instep, or low-drive, kick is the best goal-scoring kick. Master it and you can score a lot of goals.

The Lofted Instep Kick Want to kick the ball a long way? The *lofted instep kick* is the one to use. Again, this kick uses the instep. But it differs from the basic instep kick in three ways.

For the lofted instep kick, place your nonkicking foot off to the side of the ball but also a little behind it.

As you kick, keep your toes pointed toward the ground but don't aim at the center of the ball. Aim your kick lower so your toes will be slightly under the ball.

Lastly, as you make contact, lean back a little.

Those three things will make the ball sail high and far downfield.

LOFTED INSTEP KICK

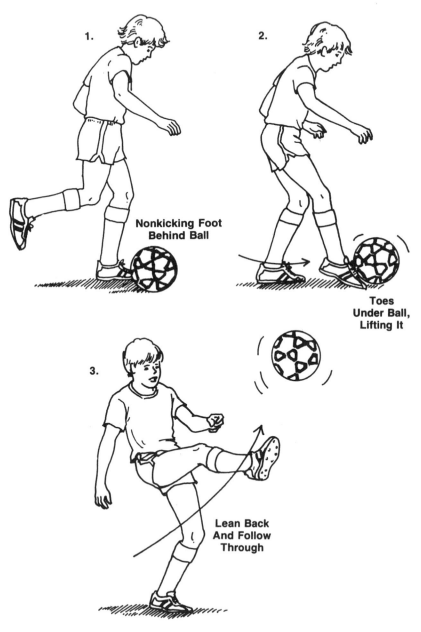

1.

Nonkicking Foot
Behind Ball

2.

Toes
Under Ball,
Lifting It

3.

Lean Back
And Follow
Through

The Chip Kick (or Lob)   The *chip kick,* or *lob,* is used to pass the ball over an opponent's head. It is also used to shoot a ball over a goalie. It is a skillful kick that takes a lot of practice to do right.

The chip kick is a lot like the lofted instep kick. The nonkicking foot is in the same position—to the side and behind the ball.

The difference is in the kicking foot. When kicking the ball, instead of pointing the toes downward, keep your toes and foot level with the ground. Aim your toes under the ball. The idea is to slip the front of your foot under the ball and scoop it up on your instep.

CHIP KICK

Toes Point At Ball When Kicking

The chip kick is not a power kick. So do not try to kick the ball hard. For this kick you need skill, not strength.

As you kick, lean back or shift your weight to the rear. This gives lift to the ball.

The Inside-of-the-Foot Kick   The *inside-of-the-foot kick* is not very powerful. But it is a very accurate kick. That is because it gets more of the foot on the ball than any other kick. It is used for short passes. It can also be used for close shots at the goal.

To do it, place the nonkicking foot a few inches away from the side of the ball. As the kicking foot approaches the ball, turn the toes outward. Aim at the middle of the ball. The ball should be hit with the inside part of your foot—along the side (near your inner ankle).

As always, keep your eyes on the ball and follow through. And don't forget to practice with both feet.

INSIDE-OF-THE-FOOT KICK

Area That Hits Ball

OUTSIDE-OF-THE-FOOT KICK

Area That Hits Ball

The Outside-of-the-Foot Kick   This difficult kick is useful for a short, soft pass to a teammate who is beside you. Put your nonkicking foot even with the outside of the ball. Bend your kicking leg. As you do, turn your toes down and slightly inward. Aim at the center of the ball. Hit it with the upper, outer side of your foot and flick it off to the side. The area of the foot you use is between the toe and ankle.

The Volley The *volley* looks great, but it's difficult for a beginner to do. The part of the foot used for a volley is either the instep or the same area used for the inside-of-the-foot kick. A volley kick is done before a ball in the air hits the ground.

Proper balance and timing are very important. Eyes on the ball are a must. As a ball in the air falls, wait until it is knee high. Lean back with arms extended. Do not swing your foot back. Swing your foot upward and make contact before the ball hits the ground.

Do not be discouraged if you miss. This kick is one of the hardest to do.

To practice a volley, toss a ball in the air and try to kick it before it hits the ground. You can also throw a ball in the air, and then try to kick it after it bounces. Kicking a ball as it falls after a bounce is called a *half-volley.*

VOLLEY

Ball
Doesn't
Hit
Ground

HALF-VOLLEY

Kicking
Ball After
One Bounce

OTHER SOCCER SKILLS:
BASIC PLAYING STRATEGIES

Shooting   What kinds of shots score goals? The answer is all kinds of shots! A well-placed chip kick can score just as easily as a powerful instep blast. To score, you must have the ball under control before you shoot. You must aim it at a target area before you shoot. You must carry out the kick you plan to use. And lastly you must get the ball past the goalie.

Experts agree the toughest shot to stop is a low drive into the corner of the goal. But any well-placed shot is hard to stop.

Of course, try to shoot the ball where the goalie isn't. Even the most powerful shot will almost always be stopped if it is aimed at the goalie.

Passing Passing is getting the ball to a teammate by kicking it. For short passes, use the inside-of-the-foot kick. For getting the ball up and over opponents, use the chip kick for short distances or the lofted instep kick for long distances.

Beginners should use low passes. These are easier for teammates to handle. Short passes are also safer than long ones. Long ones are more easily intercepted.

PASSING

Whenever you can, try to pass to an unguarded team-mate. If a teammate is moving when you pass, kick the ball a little in front of him or her. That is called *leading the player.* That way, your teammate can receive the pass in stride without stopping.

After you pass the ball, do not stop. Keep running to an open position to receive a pass. The ball may be sent back to you. In soccer, a pass followed by a return is called a *wall pass.*

When a ball is passed to you, run up to meet it. Do not wait for the ball to come to you—go to it.

Trapping In soccer, stopping and gaining control of a ball has a special name. It is called *trapping.* You can trap a moving ball with your foot, your leg, or any body parts except your arms and hands.

Trapping with the sole of the foot is the most common trap. Lift your foot off the ground. Bend your knee and point your toes up slightly. Keep your heel down. Stop the moving ball under your raised foot. Let the ball touch the ground. As it begins to bounce upward tap it back down with the sole of your foot.

TRAPPING

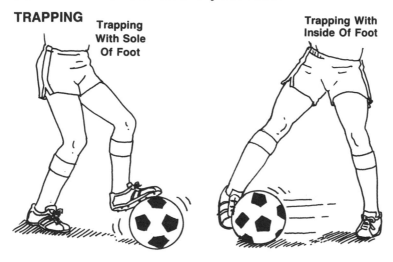

Trapping With Sole Of Foot

Trapping With Inside Of Foot

Trapping with the inside of the foot is also used quite often. Again, the foot is raised. But this time the toes stay level with the ground. The inside part of the foot is lifted slightly and turned toward the ball. The moving ball is wedged between the foot and the ground.

The chest can also be used to trap a ball in the air. Keep the body relaxed. Do not be rigid when the ball strikes you. Try to cushion it against your body so it drops in front of you instead of bouncing off.

TRAPPING

Lean Back

Dribbling In soccer, moving the ball along with short, light kicks is called *dribbling*. It is not easy. The ball must be kept under control as you move down the field.

To learn how to dribble, walk before you run. You can use either the inside or the outside of your foot to move the ball forward. But do not use your toes.

DRIBBLING

Tap the ball gently so it does not roll too far. It should not move more than a foot or two. As you walk, change feet. Dribbling with both feet is a must.

Start out slowly. When you can comfortably control the ball, move faster. Go in straight lines first. Then try weaving around. Keep switching feet as you dribble. As you get better, try changing your speed as you move.

When dribbling by an opposing player, use the foot farthest from that player to move the ball past. Keep your body between your opponent and the ball.

HEADING

Use Forehead

Heading Another way to shoot or pass a ball in the air or to get a ball away from your own team's goal is called *heading.* However, the ball is not hit with the top of your head. To head a soccer ball, use your forehead.

Do not be afraid to head a ball. The flat part of the forehead is very good for hitting a soccer ball.

When you see the ball coming, do not wait for it to hit you. You must hit it instead. Tense your neck muscles. Keep both eyes on the ball. Jump or leap at the ball with your body under control. *Use your forehead!* As you strike the ball, use your upper body or torso to give it direction. Heading is easy to learn and a great soccer tool when mastered.

Tackling In soccer, *tackling* means taking the ball away from your opponent. This is quite different from tackling in American football, where you pull a player down to the ground. That is not legal in soccer, nor is rough play allowed.

Front tackling is used when a player is dribbling at you. Get in the dribbler's path. Stand in a balanced position. Tuck your elbows in to your sides so you do not use your arms in a way that is not allowed. If the dribbler moves to your right to avoid you, use your right leg for the tackle. Stretch your foot out to knock the ball away as he or she tries to go by. If the dribbler goes to your left, use your left leg and foot.

Be careful not to be fooled by the dribbler. He or she may pretend to go right and then cut left. Also, make sure you keep your eye on the ball. The ball is what you

FRONT TACKLE

must hit with your foot. If you miss the ball and trip the dribbler, a foul will be called against you.

A *sliding tackle* is used when there is no other way to get the ball. Lots of beginners like to try the sliding tackle because it looks so exciting. But if you miss a sliding tackle, all you can do is watch from the ground as your opponent dribbles away.

A sliding tackle is like a baseball slide. You slide on the ground by tucking one leg under your body. The other leg is stretched out toward the ball. The foot of the outstretched leg kicks the ball away. Go for the ball and not for the player's feet.

SLIDING TACKLE

Remember, you can only use one foot to tackle. Tackling with two feet is illegal. So make sure your tackles are clean and legal.

Defensive Play When the other team has the ball, you must stop them from scoring. Watch where the ball goes. But stay in your area of the field. If the ball comes into your area, challenge the player who has the ball. If you are guarding a player who does not have the ball, do not allow the ball to be passed to him or her if you can help it. Remember the rules of tackling. Most important of all, stay between your goal and the player you are guarding.

For more about the defensive skills of goaltending, see pages 53-56.

Out-of-Bounds Plays

In soccer, play is stopped briefly when the ball goes out of bounds. There are three ways the ball is put back into play after it goes out of bounds.

THE THROW-IN

Do you remember what the side boundaries of a soccer field are called? They are called touchlines. To be out of bounds, the ball must roll all the way over the touchline. A ball on the touchline is not out of bounds. It can be dribbled or played.

When a ball is kicked over the touchline, the team that kicked it over loses the ball. The ball goes to the other team. The way it is returned to play is special. It is the only time during a game a player other than the goalie is allowed to pick up the ball in his or her hands. It is put back in play with a *throw-in*.

The throw-in takes place at the spot where the ball crossed the touchline. To throw the ball in, hold it in two hands. It cannot be thrown with one hand. Spread your fingers to give you more control. You must raise the ball above and behind your head. It is against the rules to throw the ball in any other way.

THROW-IN

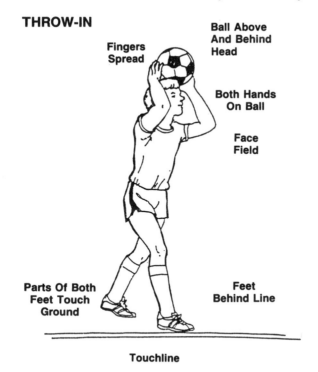

Fingers Spread

Ball Above And Behind Head

Both Hands On Ball

Face Field

Parts Of Both Feet Touch Ground

Feet Behind Line

Touchline

Face the field. You are not allowed to stand sideways. Both feet should be behind the touchline. As you throw the ball in, parts of both feet must be on the ground. It is not permitted to lift your feet or jump. Some players keep their lead foot flat and drag the toe of their rear foot as they throw. Others keep both feet flat. Some take a two-step running start and then drag the back toe.

Beginners should stand with both feet still and flat. Release the ball in one smooth motion, and continue the motion after you release it. Do not put any spin on the ball. If you make a wrong throw-in the other team takes the throw-in.

THE CORNER KICK

Suppose you are near the opposing team's goal with the ball. A player from the opposing team makes a tackle. The ball is kicked out of bounds across the end-line boundary. Your team gets the ball. But how do you put it back in play?

Your team gets a *corner kick*. A corner kick is taken from the corner area formed where the touchline meets the end line. The area is marked on a regulation field by a small quarter circle and a flag.

If the ball is kicked out near the left side of the goal, the corner kick is taken on the left side. If it goes out on the right side, the kick is from the right.

In a corner kick try to get the ball up into the air. You want to curve the ball so it lands near the goal where your teammates are waiting. This is a very hard kick for beginners. The kick used is like a lofted instep kick. Making it curve takes a lot of practice.

THE GOAL KICK

Imagine you take a shot at the goal and miss. The ball goes over the end line and out of bounds. The ball belongs to the other team. They put it back in play with a *goal kick*.

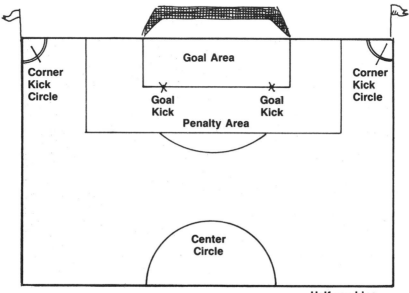

The goal kick is made from the side of the goal area where the ball went out (right or left). It is placed on the ground and then kicked away from the goal. Most often, the goalie kicks it. Sometimes another player kicks it. The player who kicks the ball must have strong legs. The ball needs to be sent far away from the goal or passed over to an unguarded player on the side. A weak goal kick sent up the middle of the field can end up as a goal for the other team.

Fun Soccer Drills

SOLO DRILLS

There will be times when you'll want to practice your soccer skills and no one will be free to join you. Four good ways of practicing soccer by yourself are wall drills, juggling, dribbling drills, and corner kicks.

Wall Drills These are good ways to practice soccer by yourself. You can practice kicking the ball against a wall inside a gym, or along the outside of a building. You can also practice trapping the ball when it bounces back.

41

Another way to use a wall is to jog alongside the wall. As you do, pass the ball to the wall. The bounce back will be like a return pass. Take the pass and continue along.

You can even practice shots at the goal against a wall. Mark off a goal area in chalk or do it mentally. Dribble in toward the wall, pick a target area, and fire. Just make sure your goal area is not near any windows or doors.

Juggling   Soccer juggling means keeping the ball in the air by using feet, thighs, and forehead.

To start, drop the ball. Use your thigh or foot to kick it before it hits the ground. Keep juggling as long as you

can. In the beginning, you will probably be able to do only a few hits before the ball drops to the ground. But you will improve with practice. So keep juggling!

Dribbling Drills These are easy to practice alone. When running laps for conditioning, you can dribble a ball as you jog.

DRIBBLING DRILL

Another good dribbling drill makes use of markers. You can use cones or paper cups as markers. Set them in a row with space between each one. Starting at one end, dribble in and around the markers, weaving in and out. Use both feet. When you reach the last marker, turn around and go back.

DRILLS WITH FRIENDS

Of course, practicing soccer with friends can be a lot more fun than practicing alone. You'll also get the chance to develop teamwork skills, something much harder to develop on your own.

Corner kicks You and a friend can practice these on a soccer field. Take turns kicking from the corner kick circle—the other person will be the goalie.

Passing This is easy to do with a partner. Just stand apart and kick the ball back and forth. You can also practice kicks and trapping.

A good way to drill with a partner is to jog up and down a field, passing the ball back and forth as you move. Do not get too far apart, however. This drill can also be done with three players.

One-on-One Drills   These are good ways to have fun and also practice. One player is the dribbler. The other is the tackler. The dribbler moves toward the tackler and tries to go by him or her. The tackler tries to steal the ball. Each time the dribbler loses the ball, the tackler becomes the dribbler. After a few minutes, take a rest. Then start again.

ONE-ON-ONE DRILL

Goalie-shooter is another good one-on-one drill for two people. A goal area is marked off. One player is the goalie. The other is the shooter. The shooter dribbles in and tries to score. The goalie tries to stop the shooter. Players can switch positions after each shot or after a number of shots.

Another variation of this drill is to use a third person. One is the defender or tackler. One is a goalie. The third is the shooter. Players take turns at each position.

TWO-PERSON JUGGLING

Two-Person Juggling   In this drill, two players face each other. They attempt to keep the ball up in the air. They kick or head the ball to each other when they can. A third person can also join in.

SOCCER KEEP-AWAY

Soccer Keep-Away   This is a fun way to practice for three or four players. Two or three players are on the outside. One is in the middle. The outside players kick the ball around. The player in the middle tries to intercept the pass. If he or she does, the person who passed the ball becomes the defender.

CIRCLE KEEP-AWAY

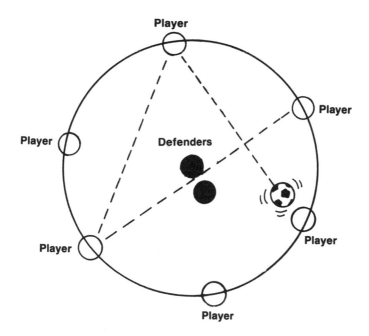

Circle Keep-Away   Five or more players form a big circle in this drill. Two players get in the middle of the circle. The outside players kick the ball across the circle, keeping it away from the people in the middle. Players take turns being in the middle or go in if their pass is intercepted.

Dribbling Relay Races   These are a way to add excitement to dribbling by turning it into a race. For dribbling relays, at least two balls are needed. The races can be run around cones or markers.

Groups of players can join in dribbling relays by taking turns. After dribbling through the course, the dribbler passes to the next player on his or her team. The first team to finish is the winner.

Shooting Contests These are a good way to practice shooting from anywhere on the field. After a goal area is marked off, place a ball in a set spot on the field (or several spots can be used, one at a time). Players take turns shooting. Each player gets the same number of shots. The player who scores the most goals from the spot (or spots) is the winner.

Soccer Positions

There are eleven players on a soccer team. Each player has a special job and a special area of the field to cover. Players do not all run to where the ball is. They stay in their areas and cover their positions.

To play certain positions, a player must have special skills. Not everyone can be a goal scorer or a goalie. Your coach will help you find the position you are best suited to play. Remember, every position is important. So play your position to the best of your ability.

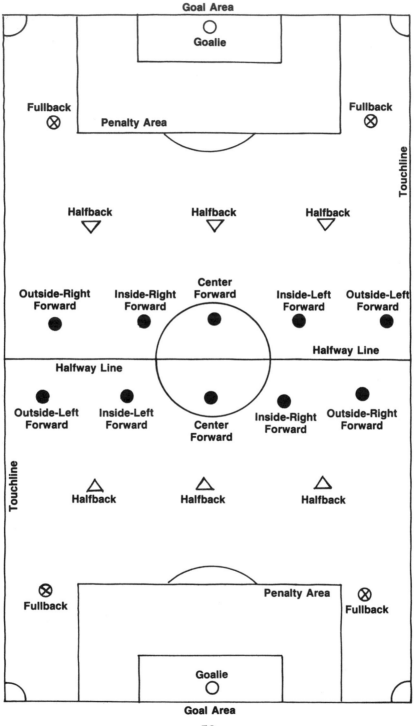

FULLBACK (OR BACK DEFENDER)

Fullbacks usually play defense and must be smart, agile, and strong. Fullbacks must also be sure tacklers and work well with the goalie. Their job is to help protect their goal.

HALFBACK (OR MIDFIELDER)

Halfbacks must be in good shape. They go up and down the field playing both offense and defense.

Halfbacks move the ball from their end of the field into the opponents' end. They form the link between the defense and the forward line, or offense.

Halfbacks are good play makers and passers. They must be quick and have fast reactions. On defense they must know how to tackle.

FORWARD (OR STRIKER)

Forwards score most of the goals. But they could not score without the help of the fullbacks and halfbacks.

Forwards must have good speed. They are expert at dribbling and trapping. Most important of all, they know how to shoot a variety of kicks. Forwards are also good headers and accurate passers.

Sometimes the two outside forwards are called *wings*. They play mostly along the touchlines.

The inside forwards are usually the best goal scorers on the team.

GOALIE

One of the most important players on a soccer team is the goalie. The goalie's job sounds simple: to stop the ball from going into the goal. But it is not simple. It is one of the hardest jobs in soccer.

A goalie is usually the tallest player on a team. Long arms and legs help him or her to reach high shots or stretch out to block shots to the side. Goaltenders must also have good, sure hands. Once a shot is stopped, a goalie must hold onto the ball so it does not roll over the line for a goal.

When a goalie has the ball in his or her hands in the goal area, no one is allowed to interfere with him or her. Kicking at a ball the goalie is holding is not allowed.

If you are a beginning goalie, stand near the goal line in the center of the net. From there you can pay strict attention to the game. Although play may not be near your goal area for a long time, you must always be ready and alert.

When the ball comes toward your end of the field, face the play. If the ball is to the left or right, move to that side and turn to face it.

When a ball is shot toward the net, keep your body between the ball and the goal. Always catch as many shots as you can. Hold the ball so it does not bounce away. If it does, the other team may get another shot at the goal.

DIVING SAVE

If you cannot catch the shot, try to knock it off to the side or over the top of the goal so it does not score. You can use your arms or fists to knock away a shot. Do not be afraid to dive to block a shot. A shot blocked or caught before it goes in the net is called a *save*. Saves do not have to look graceful. Every save that stops a goal is beautiful.

Sometimes it is necessary for a goalie to leave the net to challenge a player dribbling toward the goal. Challenging a player with the ball may force him or her to shoot from farther away. Far shots are less accurate than close ones.

HOLDING A SAVE

Any ball bouncing around the net area is a danger to the goalie. The goalie should always scoop up or pounce on any loose balls near the goal.

After making a save, the goalie must put the ball back into play. The goalie can kick or throw the ball. The goalie can also walk with the ball. But he or she can take only four steps before releasing it.

A goalie can throw the ball with one hand, like a baseball. The throw should be to an unguarded player off to the side of the field. Never throw the ball into the middle of the field.

PUTTING BALL BACK INTO PLAY

A. Goalie Throwing Ball

B. Goalie Kicking Ball

A goalie can also kick the ball by dropping it from his or her hands. Kicks go further but are not always as accurate as throws.

Goalies can help their teammates by calling out directions. A goalie is something like the field general of a soccer team.

Tips on
Regulation Play

The standard soccer game consists of two 45-minute halves. But in games involving younger players, the halves are usually thirty minutes each. An intermission of at least ten minutes is taken between halves and a break of a minute or two is taken at the midpoint of each half.

Apart from these breaks there are virtually no time-outs in soccer unless an injury occurs. Player substitutions are usually made during the short pause that follows the scoring of a goal or the ball crossing a touchline.

A goal is officially scored when the whole ball passes over the goal line between the goal posts and beneath the crossbar. Each goal counts one point, and the team scoring the most goals wins the game.

KICKOFFS

Kickoffs start the play at the beginning of the game and at the half. They also start play again after a goal. Kickoffs take place in the center circle. The ball is placed on the center spot in the center circle (see the diagram on pages 14–15).

SOCCER KICKOFF

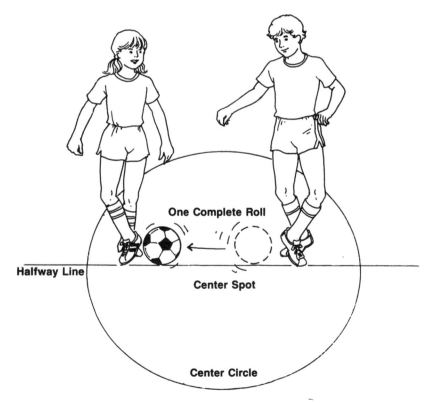

One Complete Roll

Halfway Line

Center Spot

Center Circle

During kickoffs, each team stays on its half of the field. Only players on the kicking team are allowed in the center circle. Opposing players must stand outside the center circle. This means they can be no closer than ten yards to the center spot where the ball is placed for kickoff.

Play begins when the ball makes one complete roll. Thus, a kickoff is usually a very short pass from one offensive player to another. The person who kicks off cannot touch the ball again until it hits another player.

FREE KICKS

There are two kinds of free kicks. A *direct* free kick is awarded after a serious foul. On a direct kick, a player can shoot at the goal, hoping to score.

An *indirect* free kick is awarded for a lesser offense. The kicker cannot score on an indirect kick. The ball must first touch another player.

Opposing players must be ten yards away from the ball on all free kicks. Free kicks are taken at the spot of the foul or infraction.

BREAKING THE RULES

The following offenses result in a direct free kick: kicking or striking a player; tripping; pushing; handling the ball (arms included); jumping at or holding an opponent; and charging a player from behind or otherwise charging a player in a dangerous or violent way.

These offenses result in an indirect free kick: blocking the progress of a player who does not have the ball; obstructing the goalie; being offside (see pages 61–62); and the goalie carrying the ball more than four steps.

PENALTY KICKS

A direct free kick awarded to the offensive team on the defensive team's penalty area (see pages 14–15) automatically becomes a penalty kick. The ball is placed on the penalty spot. It is a one-on-one shoot-out between the kicker and the goalie. It is one of soccer's most exciting plays.

PENALTY KICK

Goalie

Kicker

OFFSIDE

It can be very difficult to tell when an offensive player is offside. But basically the rule is: At least two players from the opposing team must be between the goal and you whenever the ball is passed forward to you on the opponents' half of the field. Otherwise, you are offside.

OFFSIDE

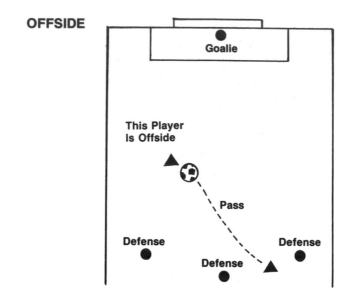

The offside rule is meant to prevent an offensive player from standing in front of the opposing team's goal and simply knocking in any long kick that comes within the area. The opposing team's goalie would be practically defenseless in such a short one-on-one situation.

ONSIDE

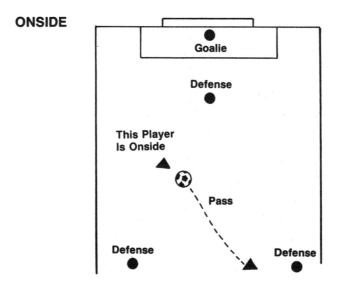

Sportsmanship

All sports are games. One team wins. The other team loses. Who wins or loses is not the most important thing. What *is* important is that you try to be the best player you can be and have fun, too.

Cheating, complaining, arguing, bragging, and pouting are not signs of a real winner. A real winner knows how to win and how to lose.

Sportsmanship is something all good soccer players should practice. A good sport is not only a winner but also a true champion.

INDEX